A Widow
Behind The Walls
And How I Got Here

Ruby Jean Robinson

WestBow Press books may be ordered through booksellers or by contacting:

WestBow Press
A Division of Thomas Nelson & Zondervan
1663 Liberty Drive
Bloomington, IN 47403
www.westbowpress.com
844.714.3454

ISBN: 978-1-6642-0925-1 (sc)
ISBN: 978-1-6642-0926-8 (e)

Library of Congress Control Number: 2020920268

Print information available on the last page.

WestBow Press rev. date: 10/26/2020

WESTBOW
PRESS®
A DIVISION OF THOMAS NELSON
& ZONDERVAN

Introduction

This book is dedicated to the widows who will read it. I want to tell you how I had to come out of the valley of sadness, loneliness and sorrows. I want you to know that God got a blessing with your name on it. Yes, it is very hard to lose your mate whether you was married for many years are a short time. But you have to tell yourself, "I got to go forward." You push through each day trying to keep a smile on your face, so your family and friends do not see the hurt that is in your heart.

I am writing this book because at this time I have come out of the valley. But there are still dark and stormy days. But I continue in prayer, asking God to order my steps. Because I know He has the plan for my life. And in God's own time and in His way, He will put someone in my life that will make me happy again. My prayer is, "Lord lift me out of my past." And please help me to put the struggle of loneliness and sadness behind me. Sometime I become so exhausted until I am tempted to give up. Then it occurred to me, I do not have to carry my past. God is not only carrying my past for me. He is also carrying me. But when you have had a good and happy marriage with a loving relationship. It is so hard to image life without it.

1

A Widow
Behind The Walls
And How I Got Here

The widow in this story is me and the loneliness I had to deal with. Friday May 4, 2018, started off like a routine Friday with Ben preparing to go to dialysis. He came into the kitchen and kept looking out of the kitchen window at the rain and said "it is a good day." Then stated "I slept better last night than I have slept in months." I thought, "Thank God things are getting better." He ate his breakfast, taken his medication and begin to put his jacket on. He dropped the car on the table came to me as always hug me tight, kissed me and said I will see you after a while. I asked him if he wanted me to drive him to dialysis? He said no and don't you go out in the rain and if you do, please be careful. Ben would leave home a little early each day he went to dialysis. His treatment was to begin at 11: AM. And at 11:15am our land line phone ring, and it was Liberty dialysis. I knew something was wrong. It was his nurse. She said his kidney doctor wanted me to meet him at Charlton Hospital emergency room after he got off his dialysis machine at 2:40 pm. I told the nurse I would come to get his keys .Because he would talk them out of getting in the ambulance. I called a neighbor to drive me to the center 5 minutes away. When I arrived the nurse came out of the treatment room and said they was giving him CPR. That he had passed out. By that time 911 emergency was entering the treatment room. 10 minutes later they asked what hospital to take him to. I told them Charlton Hospital.

When I arrived at the hospital, I was escorted to the waiting room by a Chaplin. She soon returned to take me into another private room where the doctor came in to say Ben had deceased. At that time my world crushed around me. It was hard to believe he would never be coming home to me again. How many times I left Charlton Hospital knowing I would return the next day to see him smile as I entered the room. He always required to have a hug daily and I loved the way he hugged me, he had a special tight squeeze even with the IV needle in his arm.

After leaving the hospital, when I arrived home family and neighbors came in to comfort and to see what they could do. I call the funeral home and arranged to meet with them on the following Monday 7th. To make the final arrangements for the funeral service. The service was held, Saturday, May 12, 2018, time 11: AM at our church New El Bethel Baptist church. The service was very good. The Dart transportation friends came and they had a special order of service for him. It was the Honor Guard Team. I was taken by surprise as I was escorted through the church house door. By a gentlemen that was to be my escort until the last rights was read and the family was dismissed from the grave.

There was other DART members inside the church, standing on each side of the aisles in salute to the family. There was two men standing down front. One at the head of the casket and another standing at the foot. Ben had worked for Dart for 32 years before retiring in 1995.

After the funeral I prepared to move from the resident where we had shared for 25 years. Within a short time. I got an apartment at the Franklin Park Senior Active Community. A short distant from where we lived. The **Will** was probated on June 27, 2018 and I moved into Franklin Park June 29, 2018. Only God could do this. And open such doors.

The Franklin Park apartment is beautiful and it did not take me long to mix with the other residents. But when night came I would feel so alone. I tried to read and that did not work. Only bible reading and prayers would get me through the night. It is so hard to be alone. Even God said," It's not good for the man to be alone" Genesis 2:18 NIV. I made it through the summer by staying busy going to the Walmart, Big Lot and Lowes, not always buying things but just to be among people. However I still had to face the night. I tried listen to Christian music but nothing helped. All I could do was to lay in silent and pray. There was times when I wondered if God was listening and did He see my tears as they fell from my eyes and wet my face. Yet, I knew He did because He promised He would be my everything, and I was not alone.

I used the Holidays as a pacifier 2018

I spent the Thanksgiving and Christmas with the family. Afraid to be along. As the New Year ushered in, the pain was still hard, and I start walking with a small group about 8:30 am each day. The only things got me through, was my cousin Alice would come by every day and sometime decorating my apartment. Every day I got up showed, made up my face put on my best pant, blouse and made my way out of the house. Everybody thought I was strong, but I was hurting. I was a woman with a broken heart. I often faxed a smile on my face and tried not to shed tears as I talked about while I had moved to Franklin Park senior active community. The neighbors was friendly and made sure they included me in as many activities that I wanted to participate in. We have an in house theater and once a month we go out to a different Theater. That took my mine off the pain that was in my heart doing the day. But I would try to stay up late each night talking to church members and friends until I felt like I could feel sleepy enough to fall to sleep when I went to bed. But sometime I would wake up at 3:am and pray until 7:am in the morning. My daily routine remained the same. Crying when I was alone.

May 3, 2019 which was Friday one year later after Ben passed on the (4th 2018)

That Thursday, I started crying. I thought of everything that had happen the day Ben died. I cried all night, I could not sleep. On Friday I had a real melt down and ended up in the ER with excess high blood pressure, 216/115. There was one gentlemen that lived in our area. That saved my life or maybe a stroke. I was at the Center going to help decorate for a meet and greet evening for new residents. When I told the director that my head felt funny and I was going to drive back to the house and take my blood pressure. And that gentlemen insisted he follow me to be sure I was alright. When we arrived at my apartment, he took my pressure and it was as I stated above 216/115. My niece Effie was called and she came right over and taken me to Charlton Hospital ER. They waited on me quietly and took some blood. Later I was called into the doctor's office and he said, they could not find anything that caused the elevation. I told the doctor that today, one year ago my husband died. The doctor held my hands and prayed for me. He counseled with me. He asked me what was my husband's name and age. I told him Ben and he was 89 years old at the time of death. The doctor stated that when Ben was borne God gave him an angel and that angel had watched over Ben for the 89 years. The angel knew Ben's joy, his sorrows, And how much Ben loved me. But God would not allow Ben to return to comfort me so God allowed Ben's Angel to come to comfort me tonight. And he felt that as he prayed for me.

They took my blood pressure again, and it was going down. The doctor said I could go home. I did not have stay at the hospital.

I made it through the rest of the summer, with prayers and tears every night. During the day I would leave the house and go to the mall. Or just take a walk. I was always happy to see my cousin Alice. She made regular visits to see if I was alright. I would visit the recreation center where I lived and mix with the others residents in any activities that was going on. But I was a broken widow full of sorrow, hiding much of my sad feelings. People who knew what had happen, they often would say, you are very strong. But if they could have seen inside of my heart they to would cry with me in the middle of the day. This has been very hard. And as I am writing this message now, I am being blinded with tears. But there is no other way to ease the pain. Now it is winter and the holidays are approaching. Thanksgiving I spent it with my Goddaughters and their family in DeSoto, TX where I live. For Christmas my niece Lashyon, wanted me come to Little Elm, TX and spend several days with her and my sister and family. But I decided it was time to stand own my feet no matter how hard it was. I needed healing so I can go forward. But standing your own feet took a lots of pain.

Prayers and tears. So I stayed home.

A Prayerful Decision I Had to Make

Today December 24, 2019, Christmas Eve. Lashyon and Terry Anderson her husband and my sister Clara McDaniel came by to leave my gifts and receive theirs. Later my step-son, Reginald Robinson his wife Kim and son Nicholas and Kim's sister Sue arrived to leave my gifts and to receive their gifts Also cousin Alice came by with gifts. All was well and I really enjoyed that Christmas Eve until night came and the doors were locked and I was alone. I starting thinking about Ben and wishing he was here to hold me in his arms as one of the things he loved to do. Christmas Eve was a very special time in our household, it was always love and fun. And receiving gifts was a mystery for me. Ben would hide my gifts in difference places to keep me from opening them before Eve at 12:0 clock midnight. He always knew what some of his gifts was. Because I loved going with him to Men Wear House to purchase a new suite. Ben loved to dress up and I loved to see him well dressed.

Looking around in my apartment seeing all the pictures on the wall. Remembering how I felt on the first date with Ben. We attended a Christmas Party with Dart Transit Company. He made me feel like I was the most special woman at the party. After the party we spent the night the Plaza Of America Hotel, it was great! We had only starting dating that November 1990. Before that night we was only friends; enjoying ourselves going to the Dixie House every Friday to eat fish. Ben loved to tell me jokes that made me laugh, he was so funny.

Remembering those good times. I started crying, sometime uncontrollable and praying. It seem that God did not hear my prayer. I felt all alone. I started crying and praying. Asking God to help me through the night. With the gits on a small table and a wall hanging Christmas tree above the table.

This did not mean nothing. I just wanted to fall asleep and never wake up. That was when it came to me how much I had lost and I could never love again. And did not want to think of it.

Christmas Eve night was really a sad time for me. After the family left I tried Playing on my IPad, but that was no company. I could only think about Ben and how we loved sharing gifts and how I loved cooking that caramel cake for him that was his special cake. I loved to see him smile as he entered the kitchen and saw the cake. My special thing was waiting for 12:0 clock midnight on Christmas Eve, to feel his strong arms around me and hearing him say Merry Christmas with a kiss. We always went to his oldest son for Christmas dinner. We enjoyed the dinner and afterward we played games. Life was good for me. But now I am alone and so lonely. I Loved Ben with all my heart and I received the same love from him.

December 25, 2019 Christmas Day.

I aroused at 7:15 am and I thanked God for getting me through the night. And allowing me to see another day. I said to myself "I made it with God's help." I knew it was a real break though. I want to live as a single woman facing any challenges that come my way. Knowing God will be present in my life. However when you think you have come over one hurdle, then you will be faced with another one.

New Year's Eve was no better.

That was another night I was along, I wanted God to take me home. Loneliness is hard. That was when I knew the death of someone you truly love, can make you not want to see the outcome. But the scripture came to me and I open my bible and began to read about the death of Jesus on the cross. Matthew 27:46 when God did not look upon His son dying on the cross. Death is ugly and cruel it is full of pain. At that time I began to heal from loneliness. Because loneliness has no power against prayer and faith in God. At that time it was about 9:30 pm. And a thought came to me. "You have a new spiral laying on your computer." Go get it and write all of your feelings down. So I obeyed I got the spiral and began to write about how bad I felt. I wrote every feeling of my loneliness and how I allowed myself to stay home and did not go to enjoy New Year's Eve with my niece in Little Elm, TX. About 12: pm midnight. The thought came to me, you have wrote all these things down about your feelings. What are you going to call this writing? This is how the subject came about. "A WIDOW BEHIND THE WALLS." I wrote the subject down and laid down and went to sleep.

2

January 1, 2020

The next morning, when I open my eyes, a thought ran through my mine. This is A new year and a new day, get up and go forward.

I am now 82 years Old

This is New Years, January 12, 2020

I am coming out of the valley of loneliness and sadness of being along. The valley is a hard place to travel. Even in your mine. It is dark with high mountains. Curves with crooked places; there are traveling thieves. There Satan love to steal your joy. Keep you unhappy. Your life can feel like midnight at noonday. A storm on a sunny day. Your pillow never get dry. Only prayers can get you through these loneliness days and nights. Keep praying because God has something good on the other side of this valley. And I will go forward. My mine is made up, where God want to lead me, I will follow. I know that He allowed me to go through the valley of sorrow and sadness to prepare me for what He has for me in the feature. I will wait, knowing God never fail. To any widow who lose your mate and life seen like you cannot overcome the grief. YES, you can. Prayers, and tears, and you will be given the answer and the way out of the valley. Stay in the word and on your knees.

Psalm 56: 8." Record my lament; list my tears on your scroll are they not in your record? NIV. God's protection is around the clock. He will always protect us. There is never a time we are removed from His presence, "He will not suffer thy foot to be removed: he that keepeth thee will not slumber." Psalm 121:3. KJV

Loneliness and sadness never leave you. No matter how much you pray, there are days you feel like God has turned His back on you. I call out to Him like He is in the other room. I would say "God are you in the bedroom? I am in the living room, please come up here because I am lonely." I knew God had my angel and Ben's angel standing right beside me. They was there to comfort me. But I wanted Ben. So I could not submit to the will of God. The pain in my heart will continue until I let go and let God. We suffer the pain of heartaches when we try to take control of our life; God has the plan. It is not easy to leave the past behind, when it has been a happy and good Marriage. But when death take that love one from you. You have no choice. I really miss Ben. 25 years of being married to him left many pleasant memories Labeled with love.

I really miss Ben, being married to him for 25 years he was like fresh roses to me, the life he lived was beautiful. I always told him he was God's ID. The children of God wears and ID tag. You can tell who they are when you meet them. Red was Ben's favorite color. I still put red roses on his grave. There is not a day go by that there is something that remind me of him. But I will wait on the Lord for His direction in my life. Isaiah 40: 31 (NIV) "But those who has hope in the Lord will renew their strength. They will soar on wings like eagles; they will run and not get weary, they will walk and not faint." This is the scripture that got me through many days and nights. I know if I wait, I will walked through the valley of despair. With enough strength to get through another day. Blinded by my tears made a sunny day cloudy. I though the sun was not going to ever shine again. My heart seem as though it would never stop breaking. Yet I knew only God could put the pieces together again.

I am still waiting because I know when God is ready and I can handle what He has for me. He will put another rainbow in the sky. Right now I am praising my way out of this valley of loneness and sadness.

There is a purpose

One of the things that has helped me to overcome loneliness and sadness. I began to find my purpose for what God want me to do. So I signed up at the neighborhood food pantry. I help stock shelfs and bag fruit and produce to be given out to the poor and needed. I volunteer each Thursday for 4 hours. Each Tuesday, I go bowling in the morning. And play bid whist with some of the residents in my senior community center in the afternoon. My life feel full and I do not feel so lonely. Yet I know that there will be days when I will have flash backs. I feel "when God calls you to something. He is not always calling you to success. He's calling you to obey! The success of the calling is up to Him; the obedience is up to you."

Many times we are searching for what we want in our life. But we need to spend more time searching for the peace with God. I am praying that I will find this peace as a widow. I have discovered it is hard to become a widow at an older age. Because you do not feel like doing things you are accustomed to doing at a young age. Ecclesiastes 12: 1 says "Remember now thy Creator in the days of thy youth, while the evil days come not, nor the years draw nigh, when thou shalt say, I have no pleasure in them." (JKV)

March 4, 2020 is my 83rd Birthday

This was a happy day, Satan could not over power my day. I was glad to get to this age. My Goddaughter, Deveta who was born on March the 4^{th,} we have the same date of birth. We went to Cracker Barrel restaurant for our diner. We celebrate this day each year. My second Goddaughter Debra was on a cruise. Deveta is a special child. I prayed when she was in her mother's wound, that she would be a girl. I told her mother I wanted to drive her to the hospital when it was time for the baby was to be born, God granted every wish.

March 19, 2020 Clear Out the Clutter

When I rose this morning, I decided it was time to clear out the clutter from my mine. As I set in front of the TV watching the news. Many thoughts ran through my mine. How much I missed living in the house where Ben and I shared for 25 years. Just as I often went through my closets to clear out clothes, shoes, purses, other things like old custom jewelry that filled the closets so there was no room for the things I wanted to replace the space with something new. Today my mine is being replace with a new way of living. Clear out the crying, clear out the loneliness, and the sad feeling that come and go. I got up today and made calls to shut-in members of the church and friends who maybe going through a storm. I prayed the words from, Psalm 51:10-13 (kJV). And I followed the direction from the words in the book of Habakkuk 2: 2-3. (NIV) Then the Lord replied, verse 2 "Write down the revelation and make it plain on tablets so that a herald may run with it." Verse: 3 "For the revelation awaits an appointed time; it speaks of the end and will not prove false. Though it linger, wait for it; it will certainly come and will not delay."

3

There Is a Time to Move Forward

I will wait for God to put what He want in my life. I am His child. I have to remember I needed to leave the past behind. Before I can see what God had for me in the future. Yes, it is hard to leave the past behind. When you have had a good marriage. But this marriage did not end with a divorce. God taken Ben home to live with Him. So I have no choice but to move forward. So today I went to lunch with a friend. We ate at the Bamboo Place. We had Chinese food. My friend and I enjoyed the outing and my friend said he would like to go back again and offered to take me back with him. He was not a date, we are only good friends.

I am willing to wait for the person God will put in my life. Someone who will love and care for me like Ben did. And at that time I will except that person and return his love. Until then I will just relax and go with the flow. David says "PRESERVE me, O God for in thee I do put my trust." Psalm 16:1 (JKV). I believe God is going to turn things around for me. He has a blessing with my name on it. There are days and nights I just get quite, no TV, or music I set in complete silent. So I can hear what God want to tell me. Meditation is good for the healing of the soul. I am stepping out of my past, not looking back. Looking back can make you fearful and faithless. However, I am not trying to look to far ahead. I just need a daily walk with the Lord. I need a new revelation every day. I had to learn in order to step out of my past was to take life a day at a time. Because waking with Jesus is an ongoing process. We have to stay in a spiritual frame of mind.

March, 2020, the Coronavirus (COVID 19) has plagued the global world. Many people are in a panic and they are gathering everything unto themselves. The store shelves are bare. Vegetable bins are bare. I am seeing how people will act in a time of crisis. On March 16, 2020, I went to the Kroger's neighborhood store and went to the vegetable bin and all the vegetable was gone except one lonely stark of collard greens. So I taken a look at it and laughed remembering how it felt to be Left alone. So I said to that stark, I know how you must feel. I picked it up and said, I will take you home with me. I could not help but to laugh about what I had said to a stark of collard greens. But that was one of my healing jokes.

This is my lonely stark of collard greens, however I got two meals from this stark. On Thursday March 19, 2020 I visited the Walmart Supermarket and there was another joke that made me laugh. I could not find no eggs and there on the shelf was one lonely carton of egg beaters sitting alone, so I said to it, I know how lonely it is to be left alone, so I will take you home with me. God will give you joy and self-entertainment, just see and look around you, and see what He has in your sight as you travel through the valley.

Going Forward Out of the Valley

Through prayer and spiritual growth, I am coming out of this valley. I do not have to stay here. God showed me the path of life. David said, verse 1-6 "The Lord is my shepherd, I shall not want He makes me to lie down in green pastures, he leads me beside quiet waters, and he restores my soul. He guides me in the paths of righteousness for his name's sake. Even though I walked through the valley of the shadow of death, I will fear no evil, for you are with me; your rod and staff, they comfort me. You prepare a table before me in the present of my enemies. You anoint my head with oil; my cup overflows. Surely goodness and love will follow me all the days of my life, and I will dwell in the house of the Lord forever. Psalm 23: 1-6 (NIV).

I always ask God for His wisdom and directions. And each day I try hard to encourage myself. Knowing that God is my shepherd. And He really will restore my spirit and my strength, if I only ask. I Meditate at the beginning of each day and then ask Lord what can I do today to grow spiritually. My simple prayer is, Lord let me bless someone or be a witness for you and tell some lose soul you can save any one. If there is another widow going through the valley of sorry, loneliness because you have lost your husband and especially at a middle age or older age as I am now and have to live alone. This is not easy. However, life is not a bed of roses, and Someone said it want be easy. But keep going forward, there is light and joy at the end of this valley. Keep believing the sun will shine again.

4

Reflecting On My Happy Years Before I became a Widow

Now that I am out of the valley. I claim the victory God has given me. I am able to reflect back on the first date with Ben Robinson Jr. Tonight Ben is taken me to a party at the Plaza of America Hotel down town. This is a Christmas party given by his job. Dallas Area Rapid Transportation Company. Ben always made me feel so special and treated me that way. After many months of being friends, now we are lovers. Ben was so easy to love because he showed so much compassion. We both had lost our mates early that year 1990. So we decided to date and see where things will lead us to.

I met many of Ben's friend and co-workers that night, being with Ben was great. I was so excited to be invited to the party. Ben seem to be excited to introduce me to his friends and co-workers. I had purchased the special dress and jewelry to look and feel special. Ben gave me a beautiful corsage corsage to wear on my wrist. We had a great time. Ben had reserved a room for us to stay at the hotel after the party. It was so good to find someone who showed so much love and compassion. Ben really knew how to capture my heart. He did it with love and how he cared for me and our relationship. I could depend on him and what he said. Most of all he loved to tell jokes and that kept me laughing. He never disappointed me and was always on time for our date

Ben and I had a lot in common. We loved to talk late at night on the phone. We both loved going to church and attending parties. Most of our conversation was about our families and jobs. Ben loved working for DART. He said he and three other men was among the first black employees to drive for the Dallas transits company before DART purchased it.

Loving Ben was easy, he always had a smile on his face. He was just the kind of man I knew I could be happy with. However, I know now that he was the man sent from God. God always give us good gifts, and place people in our life that make us happy and the relationship will last through the years. God gave me that handsome man and I thank God for the 25 years we was together. Yes, his home going has been hard for me. He really belonged to God

I Did Not Know This Would Last For A 25 Year Love Journey.

This picture was taken at a Christmas dinner at the home of Mr. Robbie Thomas and Rosie Thomas. Ben was a very loving man. And wherever we went he showed this kind of affection toward me. This is how I knew he truly loved me. And he showed this kind of love and affection through out of our 25 years.

Ben spoiled me and I will have a hard time going into another relationship unless it is in God's will. I do not know what God have in His plan for my life I just have to trust Him. My prayer is that I will not be afraid of the process that God has for me. I pray that I will be prepared to move forward in God's will. And except the things He want me to do. Yes, I really miss Ben and the things we enjoyed doing together. But we will meet again someday.

This is the Ben I will always remember. Our weekends was always special for us. We are resting after a walk at Bauchman Lake. What made it special, Ben was a pleasant person always telling jokes that was so funny, I could not help but keep laughing at each one. We really enjoyed our relationship. However we did not know what God had planned for our lives. I met Ben as a friend he impressed me a lot. One of the thing that was so funny, after many months going to Friday night dinners. One evening he asked if anyone was calling on me. I said no. and I asked him if he was interested in anyone. He replied no. Two weeks later he asked if we could call on each other. Because the way I enjoyed him I did not hesitate to yes! It was so nice to have someone who cared so much for me. Ben was a God fearing man. He enjoyed serving as a deacon in his church and being a family man. We both had been married, our mates died in the same year 1990 a few months apart.

Ben was married for 41 years with five children and I was married for 18 years and no children. Only one God-daughter Deveta Williams. Who is a loving Christian woman at this time.

A Surprise Birthday Party

Ben and I ate at the Dixie House every Friday night. He had a corner table that he loved to be served at. As always Ben loved surprising me with things. One Friday night he had invited two of my best friends for a surprise birthday party for me. How he did it, really surprised me.

This was a very much a surprise. I did not know that he had called Diann and OJ to join us. Ben and Diann had wrapped their presents in different things. Ben had all of his presents in a small brown shipping box and Diann and OJ had theirs wrapped in an M&M box. We had a very good time that night but dinner was still fish dinners with a small cake. Diann was one of my co-worker at Thomas Jefferson High School. She was a lovely person and she truly loved Ben. She always said it look like he made me happy and she liked that. It was not hard for Ben to like my friends and he was liked and admired by them. Wherever we went he was comfortable with my friends and family. Some of my nieces called him Uncle Ben long before we were engaged. Ben was the love of my life. My heart always skipped a beat to see him pull in my driveway.

5

25 Years of Love that Will Never Die.

After many months of enjoying each other we decided to drive to Marshall, Texas to meet my parents and sister. They loved him right away. And he loved my family; so we made many weekend trips to Marshall to spend time with the family. March 2, 1991 my mother had a stroke and twelve days later she died. Ben stayed by my side throughout the whole funeral arrangement and service. It was his care and compassion that helped me to trust his love for me.

After mother's death we continued to travel to Marshall to visit with my sister and father. Our love grew stronger as time went by. On one of our trips from Marshall, as we traveled along interstate 20, near Lavender Road exit I was about to take a picture of a beautiful scenery along the interstate. When Ben said to me, I am going to marry you one day and I do not want you to tell anybody. That was so funny, I could not stop laughing until we was almost in Tyler, Texas. I do not remember telling him "Yes," It was three years later after we was married. I said to him one night. How did we end up married because you never proposed to me? Ben stated, you do not remember I proposed to you on interstate 20. I thought he should have got on his knees with a ring to ask me "Will you marry me?" But Ben was always doing things to surprise me. Ben was a person that I could not be too sad around for long. These are some of the many memories that I cherish. Knowing that good memories are good for your health. Yes, there are days you will get lonely and even cry but get that picture album and relive those precious days and times.

One night Ben and I was talking on the phone when he said, we will be getting married in July and go on a cruise for the honeymoon. I was so in love with Ben until it did not matter which one of us made the final decision about getting married. I was just ready to be his wife. I could not wait until the next day to tell my best friend Diann that the month had been set for Ben and I would be getting married. Diann was excited and we started making plans where the wedding would be. At Bethany Baptist Church or a wedding chapel. And what color my bride maids would wear. I knew I would wear white. We finally decided on pink.

Ever since I was a young lady I dreamed of having a wedding and my dress would be white with a chiffon train. I did not want to purchase a wedding dress. So I went to a wedding gown renal shop. And the second dress I pulled from the rack, was that perfect dress. The bride maid dress was pink. Since Ben's daughter was the only bride maid, she was satisfied with the lovely pink dress and to be my bride maid.

Diann and I searched out some wedding chapels and found one in the area. I really did not want to have the wedding in the church since it is much more expenses. We found the Chapel of the Bell nearby our neighborhood. From that time I spent lots work getting wedding invitation printed, and a list of guests to be invite. Ben and I decided on the date and time in July the wedding would be. We decided on Saturday July 11, 1992. The time would be 3:PM. Ben and I went to the wedding chapel to check out everything we had to do and finalize the date. When we arrived at the chapel, we loved the area and how the chapel looked. The court yard grounds was covered with cobblestone and there was an area to have a wedding party if you wanted to.

Making Plans to Marry the Love of My Life

All I could remember after Ben said he was going to marry me someday, I just wanted to be his wife. After some months, we was making plans for July 11, 1992. We plan to share our honeymoon on a cruise. I was really excited and told my best friend, Diann that Ben had asked me to marry him. Diann was excited, and we set down to decided where the wedding would be held. If I would use the Bethany Baptist church where I was a member or we would look for a wedding chapel. That would be less expensive. Diann and I searched and found The Chapel of the Bell a wedding chapel that was near our neighborhood. Later Ben and I visited the chapel and we was excited how the chapel looked; and also the wedding plans they offered.

We was also satisfied with Pam, who was the owner and wedding planner. She coronated everything according to our wish. Our colors was white and pink. The contract offered the use of a reception room, cake, and punch. And champagne for the wedding toast. However we decided on ginger ale.

In the contract, everything was furnished all we had to do was to bring our wedding clothes. She showed us what the wedding drill should look like. Since my father's health would not let him walk me down the aisle. She suggested that Ben would meet me halfway the aisle and escort me back to the altar. We practice lighting the unity candle.

For our wedding day, Pam dressed the chapel and it was beautiful. With white and pink bows attached to the seats. Members of Ben's family participated in the wedding. I wore white and my bride maid wore pink. Ben's oldest son, Reginald Robinson was his best man and one of his daughters was my bride maid. Another daughter assisted me with getting dressed and making sure my make-up looked good. We had invited 100 guests to the wedding. That was our family and co-workers. Ben's co-workers was from Dallas Area Rapid Transit Company. And my co-workers was from Dallas Independent School District. The wedding was held Saturday, July 11, 1992 at 3: PM. It was a very hot day and Ben and I was concerned that all our guest would not show up due to the heat. But they all came and everything went well.

This was the greatest moment in my life. Meeting the man I truly loved at the altar. I was so happy knowing I would spend the rest of my life loving him and supporting him in every need. And I had no doubt about his love and support. Because I knew Ben was a man sent from God to be my husband. Although it seem like my eyes was closed, they was not. I was looking down trying not to step in the hem of my wedding dress. But my heart was open for Ben.

I had a feeling our marriage would last until one of us was called home by God to spend eternity in Heaven. Ben was a loving person who required much attention and affection. That was one of the things we had in common. So going to the altar to meet him and become his wife was everything I wanted in life. I knew the journey we was about to take would be the right one for both of us. You will never get too old to fall in love and desire to become one with someone God put in your life. It is not the will of God for us be alone. Ben and I was still young enough to remarry and have a good life. So this is the way it all ended for 25 years. With the man I love.

Reginald with his dad in the wedding dressing room. Reginald has always been a great support to his father. He was faithful and no distant was too far for him to travel to be by his father's side. Reginald was not only support to his father, he was also one of my co-workers. I knew that was a good time to be by his father's side. When Ben was excited, he would get emotional when he was excited or sad.

That day was a day we knew when we came out of our dressing rooms it would a large audience waiting to wish us a happy life together. I was also excited and did not know how I would act. However, when it was time for us to put the rings on each other's hand, I was really nervous and though Ben was giving me the wrong hand. I kept pushing the hand down, then the Pastor took the ring and held up Ben's hand that the ring was to go on. That really bought laughter from our guest. When the Pastor was reading our vows, Ben starting sweeping my hands and looked like he wanted to cry. But quickly composed himself. The pastor was my pastor where I was a member at the Bethany Baptist Church.

After my pastor, Rev. Marke Toles had read the wedding vows about how we was to love, cherish and honor each other. He told Ben, "Now you can salute your bridge," This felt good and right that we should seal our life together with a kiss.

Now we have become one from this day forward we will be one against everybody and anything in the world. We pledged to be true and committed to each other. This commitment lasted for 25 years until God called Ben home May 4, 2018.

Now I am Ruby Jean Robinson

This was so much fun to see which of the ladies would be the next bride. That was a good feeling to see all of them reaching for the bouquet. That was a great day for me because I had been given peace and a man that I knew he loved me above all thing except God. As I write this book telling others about how it feel to be given a gift from God. This day, I have another family and so many friends who stayed by Ben and I through the years and many was there through his sickness to comfort him and by my side at the end of our 25 years.

There is nothing like being loved and cared for and knowing where your joy come from. That it is given to you by God and He had our lives planned from the beginning. Some of our family and friends has moved to other parts of the world and some has passed on and waiting for us in Heaven. At this time I am writing this book, Ben has passed on and waiting for me and I will see him someday and share the joy with him and our Heavenly father.

So I keep pressing forward doing the will of God and serving wherever He want me to. Teaching and encouraging my family and friends to continue to walk with God and be thankful for His blessings.

This is the wedding table setup in the reception room.

This is our beautiful wedding cake.

Ben and Ruby cutting their wedding cake.

Ben is cutting his bridegroom cake. That he requested to be special made by one of our best friend by Mrs. Arva Mays. It is a caramel cake. He love that cake.

Ben and Ruby sharing their wedding cake with each other.

It felt so good to be making a toast to Ben who is now my husband.

Millie Ferguson, Ruby Jean, Ben Robinson and Floyd Ferguson

These are our good friends, Floyd and Millie Ferguson. Floyd taken and processed all our wedding pictures. The Ferguson are a lovely couple. Wherever you see Floyd, you will see Millie. They loved to travel and Floyd loved taking pictures. This picture was taken July 11, 1992. I am very sad as I am putting this picture in my book. "A Widow behind the Walls." Now I am the only one still alive in this picture. Today July 14, 2020. I am writing and reflecting and remembering the happy life with Ben and all our friends.

I can only say God is and awesome God. When you service Him from your youth He will give you peace and joy in your old age. Yes, you will from time to time get truly lonely and sad for the absent of the one you love. But knowing he is resting in the arms of God and not suffering from the sickness that had taken away some quality of life he had enjoyed for years. However God allowed him to have a family of five children and 25 year of a happy remarriage to me. I am truly grateful.

CHAPTER

6

Going On A Honeymoon With The Love Of My Life

Ruby Jean Robinson & Ben Robinson Jr

Ben and I are about to board our ship to the Bahamas Island where we will spend three days. This was the first cruise for the both of us. We sailed with the Carnival cruise line, from Miami to Freeport, and on to the Bahamas Island.

We enjoyed the Carnival cruise line because there was a lots to things to do on the ship and we enjoyed the things we saw on shore. It was interesting to see how the people lived on the Island. It was so differing from our life style in the Unite State.

Tonight we will celebrate and take pictures with the Captain on the ship this is another night I will never forget. There is nothing like being with the handsome man you are in love with out on the sea. We attended many of the shows on the ship. Because we was newlywed, the crew that serviced us in the dining room serenaded us along with the other people that was seated at the table with us. They also gave us a small wedding cake. I was so excited with the hostility of all the crew members on the ship. We received very good service. There was places to go shopping and we both did a lot of that. We decided to take advantage of everything that was available during the three days. Tomorrow we will go ashore to see what the Island look like.

Today we went into one of the parks on the shore and a young boy came to us and asked if we wanted him to take our picture. It was so funny when the young boy approached us and asked if he could take our picture. I hesitated and he said Ma'am I will not take your camera. So we allowed him to take this picture. Ben also saw this is one of the ways the young boy was making money, so he gave him $5.00 for his service.

We later taken a buggy ride through part of the Island. I was not impressed with the Island. There was so many broken sidewalks, people selling tee shirts. In the parks. The shirts was lying on the ground. Some of the tee shirt merchants had theirs hanging on side of buildings. Down by the sea shore there was more young boys diving into the ocean as travelers throw coins in the ocean, they would dive in to collect the coins.

After the three days in the Bahamas, we returned home back with our families and jobs. Our new life together was interesting. We continue to attend church and special events. Ben was a deacon and an usher he also served with the Men Ministry in our church. And I still enjoy teaching Sunday school in the Junior Department and serving as one of the teachers in the Women Day Mission Ministry and a teacher for the Deaconess Ministry. I also serves on the Senior Usher Board. I really enjoy being on the church Email Ministry; for the Member to

Member Ministry in the church. Ben and I had a lot of things we enjoyed doing together. In our neighborhood we enjoyed volunteering with our (HOA) Home Owners Association and the Adopt- The Street Program.

We continued traveling to Marshall, Texas to visit my father and sister. In 1995 Ben retired from (Dart) Dallas Area Rapid Transportation Company. And he awarded himself with a 1995 SRX Cadillac. I retired in 1996 and he taken me on a 7-day cruise to Puerto Rico. We cruised with the Caribbean cruise line. Our destination was to visit San Juan and St. Martin Island. We have really had a happy life. Ben was a happy man and always let me know how much he loved and appreciated my love and care for him.

As life will have it, there will always be a change after many years in your marriage. In 2013, Ben health failed him. He had a kidney failure and had to go on dialysis for the last four years of his life. He still continued to be happy and positive about things around him. Because I loved him so much, I gave up all activities and dedicated my time to taking care of him. Through all the times he spent in the hospital and Rehabilitation. He always praised God.

A Pandemic Called Coronavirus

Now it is March 2020 and I am just getting over the lonely feelings I have struggled with for months. The next hurdle is here! A pandemic called Coronavirus has spread global wide. People are getting sick and dying by the thousands. My question is, "what do I do now?" We are asked to stay home. Shopping malls beauty shops, barber shops, bowling alleys theaters and all kinds of business are closed. Even our recreation center has closed and we cannot meet for bid whist card games weekly and other activities.

I started walking two miles three times a week in the senior community where I live. Except for the location of my unit I would go crazy. My unit is located near an open field with lots of trees and wild flowers. It is incredibly quiet here. And since we all have to stay home. Not many people are out during the day. At night it is like a cemetery and the car look like tombstones parked. Everything is really quiet at Bridgemoor Active Senior Community.

I know this will not last forever. God is giving us a recess period so we can slow down and pray and to check ourselves and listen to Him. God has always made changes to His world for the better. So we need to be patience and get some much needed rest and refocus on our lives. Right now we are living in a Microwave Society where we want everything right now. Technology has separated the family. Even the cell phone get most of our time. The mothers give their babies a tablet to play with for a pacify. The daily meal is a frozen entrée. Table grace, bed side stories and prayers are not taught to the children any more. Community football games and practice has replaced the Mid-week services. Our children Sunday school class rooms are almost empty. God want our attention and want us to return to Him.

I Am Refocusing On My Life These Days

I refuse to believe the lies that Satan is trying to tell me and trying to enter my mine. He want to steal my joy. I refuse to be locked into the spirit of sadness and loneliness. Through my daily reading and praying without ceasing. As stated in 1.Thessalonians 5: 17. Verse 5:18 Paul said "In everything give thanks: for this is the will of God in Christ Jesus concerning you." (kjv) I told myself it is alright to cry. After two years of Ben's death, yes I still cry and get depressed but I have learned that crying is a part of healing for the soul. To the widows who will lose your love one. Yes the pain in the heart is so hard until it seem that nothing is going to give you some ease. I would cry out aloud asking God to stop the pain in any way He would see fit. Sometime I just sit silent taking deep breaths waiting for the answer from God.

After I fall asleep and wake up the answer would be in my mine. The spirit would move through my memory. Yes, God is here! And He know how much you are hurting and His way is not too hard. God want you to trust Him. Take a look at your life and think of everything, and think positive at all thing that make you sad and lonely. Knowing there is only 24 hours in a day. Twelve hours you are awake. And the other twelve hours you are asleep and not having to deal with live and thing around you. You are in the hands of God.

I do not understand all the reasons for the Coronavirus and while the entire universe is suffering and is in mourning with the loss of many love ones. But God are saying I am stronger than you are. Your burdens are not overwhelming to me.

I will carry them for you. I cannot tell you when all these things will end. But when it end, I believe we will be stronger in our faith again.

Being closed off in my home, I have time to listen to God, and discover my own self. For me I have learned that there are things I thought I needed they do not matter anymore. I had just enough to live with day by day. There are clothes, shoes in the closets, some are new but I do not have no place to wear them.

I will soon have another birthday and will be 84 years old. I am thankful for the years and a portion of health that God has granted me. Yes being a widow, I am living alone, and every day is not sunshine there are lonely storms; and thoughts go through my mine that there is not much fun being old, alone and living with only memories of the past life. So to keep moving forward I start working on some projects that get me through each day.

A note to the young people. Do not waist your years in idol time. For live is given to us to have a purpose for each day. Helping others that cannot help themselves. Taking care of the seniors in your community, nursing homes. Or just given a smile to a stranger you meet on your way. The days you share with others will revisit you in your old age.

Keeping looking to the hills where all our help come from. Yes, to widows young or old, there is nothing wrong with hoping for another mate as long as you have asked God to let that mate be sent from Him. Stay focus this to will pass.

SCRIPTURES USED IN THE BOOK

The Author's Note

I am writing this book because I want to tell my story on how hard it was for me to overcome the loss of my husband. Who had been so good and kind to me throughout the 25 years of our marriage. With God and Ben I had a full happy life. and writing has been a source of healing.

Delight thyself also in the Lord;
and He shall give thee the desires
of thine heart. Psalms 37: 4 KJV

Biography

Ruby Jean Haggerty-Robinson born in Waskom, Texas a small East Texas town, March 4, 1937. My parents moved to Jonesville, Texas.

My Faith: Baptist: I was baptized at the age of 12 and became a member of Old Border Baptist church in Jonesville, Texas.

Education: I attended Hart Elementary School. The highest grade they went to was the 9th grade. I later moved to Dallas, Texas where I earned a GED and continued my education at El Centro Community College in Dallas, Texas. 1979 I earned an Associate Degree of Secretary Science.

Employment: My first job after leaving school was with the Verhalen Nursery in Scottville. Texas. I worked in the nursery garden, pruning and potting Plants. After five years, I moved to Dallas, Texas 1956. And was employed by Holiday Laundry and Dry Cleaners for 13 years. And Texas Scottish Rite Children Hospital for 4 years.

1972 employed by Dallas Independent School District for 23 years and retired in 1996.

Hobby: Reading, writing, Playing Bid Whist and serving as one of the email members for my church.

Printed in the United States
By Bookmasters